Pr...

India's First Woman President

"Fantastic! Fantastic!" was how Dr. APJ Abdul Kalam reacted on hearing that Pratibha Patil would be taking over from him as the next President. On July 25, 2007 history was created as Pratibha Patil was sworn in as President of the Republic of India–the first woman ever to hold the highest office of this country. Table-tennis champion, qualified lawyer, social reformer and career politician, who was relatively unknown till just a few months ago, Pratibha Patil today is a household name – a name that will be recorded in the annals of history.

This book provides some glimpses into the life of Pratibha Patil – the major influences that shaped her life and her political journey of thirty-four long years.

Written by Ritu Singh, a postgraduate in History, educated at St. Mary's Convent, Nainital and La Martiniere Girls' College, Lucknow, Ritu has over twelve years of experience in writing, editing and translating for children and adults.

President Pratibha Patil
India's First Woman President

Ritu Singh

Price : Rupees Ninety-five only (Rs. 95.00)

First Edition : August 2007 © Rajpal & Sons
ISBN : 978-81-7028-705-6
PRESIDENT PRATIBHA PATIL : India's first Woman President
by Ritu Singh

Rajpal & Sons, Kashmere Gate, Delhi-110006
www.rajpalsons.com
email : mail@rajpalsons.com

Contents

The Shifting Sands	7
A Winner is Born	15
The Call of Duty	21
The Early Days	29
A Lasting Partnership	35
Pratibha Tai	43
Entry Into Politics	49
The Governor of Rajasthan	57
The President's Chair	67
Celebration Time	77
The Republic's First Servant	83
Patil and Clinton	91
Women in Power	97
A Defining Moment	107

1

The Shifting Sands

My address is like my shoes. It travels with me. I abide where there is a fight against wrong.

—Mother Jones

1

She loved coming here, more so in the summer, away from the dust, grime and scorching heat of the desert sands. Even though her work travelled with her, the peace and quiet of this heavenly place did wonders to rejuvenate the mind and senses. Driving up the Aravalli range, one of the oldest in the world, on the curved road leading to this haven, she had never failed to be fascinated by the peculiarly shaped rocks and strong winds that marked this dry region. And, once atop at 1219 metres above sea level, she could barely wait to alight from the car on to the blessed soil of the only hill station in Rajasthan, and for that matter, in the entire north-western India.

Blessed it truly was, both by nature and the gods. The lush green hills forested with tall trees and flowering shrubs, and the gushing waterfalls and calm lakes, were a soothing sight for sore eyes. The very first breath of the cool air was enough to make one worship life in all its wonder. And, even if you were not of a spiritual bent of mind, the sound of the bells from the beautiful Dilwara temples of the eleventh and thirteenth centuries, visited by tourists from all over the world, made you feel that indeed there was a guiding hand somewhere above.

Ah! Mount Abu – legendary home to thirty-three crore gods and goddesses, once said to be inhabited by numerous rishi-munis – the sages of wisdom. According to a legend, once, sage Vashishth's cow Nandini was trapped in a deep gorge and could not free herself. The sage appealed to Lord Shiva for assistance. The Lord sent Saraswati, the divine river, to help flood the gorge so that the cow could float up. Wanting to ensure that such mishaps did not recur, Vashishth asked the youngest son of Himalaya, the king of mountains to fill the chasm permanently. This he did with the assistance of Arbud, the mighty snake. This spot came to be known as Mount Arbud, and later came to be known as Mount Abu. Prior to Independence, Mount Abu had been leased to The East India Company by the Maharaja of Sirohi. From then till 1947, it had served as the headquarters for the Resident of Rajputana, as well as a sanatorium for troops and thereafter, it became Rajasthan's summer capital

Somehow, all of this combined to give one a feeling of safety and security. Particularly if you were sitting in the political hot seat of power, as she was. Whatever the Constitution might say about the ceremonial powers of a state governor, it was no cakewalk. One had to tread very carefully on the hot sands of time. As the Governor of Rajasthan,

Pratibha Patil was only too well aware of this truth, having recently weathered the Gujjar storm.

Her thoughts returned to Raj Bhavan, that big colonial bungalow of the Jaipur royalty which was now her official residence. It was on November 8, 2004 that she had taken the solemn oath in English-administered by the Chief Justice of the Rajasthan High Court, Y.R. Meena, in the presence of Chief Minister Vasundhara Raje and Speaker of the Rajasthan Assembly, Sumitra Singh.

It had been a first for her, and for Rajasthan too when in November 2004, she had become the sixteenth Governor of the state, and its first woman Governor, succeeding Madan Lal Khurana. It also made her the second politician, after Vasantdada Patil, from Maharashtra to hold this office.

It had been a solitary and somewhat lonely stay of three years. She had of course had to shift from Maharashtra to Jaipur, while her husband had continued to stay on in Amravati, visiting her once a month. Her son, Rajendrasingh, who lived in Mumbai, and daughter Jyoti Rathod, an electronics engineer based in Pune, were able to come and see her once a year. Unlike her predecessors she did not hold parties or any musical soirees. As Governor, Pratibha Patil lived simply, incurring little expenditure on herself, so much so that sometimes the budget even lapsed.

Even the Raj Bhavan had undergone little physical change. It was a simple building anyway, the only extravagance being the grand old chandeliers. As Governor she had made no changes, added no furniture, to the extent that even the guest houses retained their old and sometimes poor furnishings. The swimming pool remained without water. All of this reflected the state's first lady's simple, even austere style of living. According to the cook, Laxman Raj, "Raj Bhavan was a vegetarian establishment during Patil's tenure. She preferred a simple breakfast of milk and toast. Lunch and dinner were chapatis and vegetables, curd and rice."

Governor Pratibha Patil did not entertain many guests. Even when she did, the menu remained simple. Once, when her husband, Devisingh Shekhawat, was visiting, the cook had asked, "Madam, what shall I cook today?"
She had answered, "The usual, of course. Why do you ask?"
Hesitatingly, the cook had said, "But, Madam, I thought something special. Sir might like..."
Smiling, she had simply shaken her head.

Thinking of the cook brought her back to the present. Now, sipping her tea unhurriedly in the lawns of her official residence in Mount Abu, a smile played about her lips as she thought to herself. "I must bring them here some day soon, when I'm free from the cares of the state. The pages of history would surely come alive for them. How they devour knowledge! Like sponges that could never run dry."

What was it that had triggered the thought of her grandchildren? It must have been the young girls at the school she had visited a few days ago in Alwar. Since her visit to Alwar, she had often thought of her two granddaughters - it had been so long since she last met them. Childhood came and went by so quickly, leaving little time to realize how precious it is. How much she missed them...

"Please, Aji, when will you play table-tennis with us? You promised...please," persisted Nilima, one of her granddaughters.
"I'm too old for a game now. But yes, I do have some tricks up my sleeve!"
"Really? Talking of sleeves, Aji, why do you always wear these old-fashioned, buttoned full-sleeve blouses? Don't you feel hot?"
She had laughed at that, "Actually, no. Cotton is cool, you know, even when it covers your whole skin. In fact, it protects you from sunstroke. Haven't you seen the big turbans the Rajasthani men wear? That's what helps them to work out in the sun without feeling faint."
"We understand all that, Aji, but we want to know more about you. When you were table-tennis champion, what did you wear for your tournaments? And how did it feel, winning trophies all the time? Come on, tell us more, Aji."

The memory of the persistent nudging by her grandchildren transported her back in time, to her own younger days, and to that very special winning day...

13

2

A Winner is Born

Winning isn't everything, but the will to win is everything.

—Vince Lombardi

2

"Shhhh... there he comes," whispered the girls as the Principal stepped on to the stage. He stood before the podium, papers in hand, his glasses just about balanced on the edge of his long nose. Head slightly bent, eyes looking over the rim, he gave a quick, stern glance at the excited, restless student audience assembled in the college hall. Then he gave a slight cough, as most principals do before making an important announcement.

"God! I can't wait any longer. Why doesn't he get on with it?" whispered a girl in the back row. As if he had heard the remark, the head of Moolji Jaitha College, Jalgaon, Maharashtra, suddenly beamed and said: "I am proud to announce that once again, for the fourth year running, the table-tennis championship trophy goes to... our very own PRATIBHA PATIL! Congratulations Pratibha! Please..."

The next words were drowned in the thundering applause of the students, clapping and cheering at the top of their voices. "THREE CHEERS FOR PRATIBHA, HIP HIP HURRAY! HIP HIP HURRAY! HIP HIP..." The teachers too were all smiles, for a change!

In the middle of the crowd, the proud winner of the moment was nearly lifted above the heads of her classmates. Of medium height, long hair plaited neatly, wearing plastic-framed spectacles, the sober but confident Pratibha waved to her friends in thanks.

The Principal tapped on the mike to get the attention of the students and said, "I request Pratibha to come on stage and accept the trophy." As she made her way to the front, being hugged and thumped on the back in turn, Pratibha felt a great satisfaction in bringing honours to her college again.

The camera lights flashed as she shook hands with the Principal and lifted the trophy for all to see. "Well done, Pratibha. We are very proud of you. And, there is yet another interesting piece of news." As the voices and cheers quietened, the Principal continued, "You will be happy to learn that Pratibha has been selected to participate in an international table-tennis tournament in the UK. Give her a big hand, ladies! And, in celebration of this very special moment, we have decided to go on a picnic today! The buses will be waiting at the college gate at 11 o'clock."

Hardly believing their luck, the young girls dispersed to collect their belongings for the outing. It was indeed a special day in the history of this college, which had been set up in 1945 with just about 166 students. It was the oldest college in the North Maharashtra region, affiliated to the North Maharashtra University. The students were rightly proud to belong to this institution, popularly known as MJ College, which had crossed many milestones in its time. Pratibha and her friends enjoyed every moment spent on the beautiful campus spread over 25 acres in Jalgoan. They had a variety of courses to choose from – Science, Commerce, Arts – and physical development, of course, was much encouraged. Pratibha was passionate about sports – be it table-tennis, kho-kho, kabaddi...

As she slung her bag over her shoulder, a friend asked, for the hundredth time, "How do you do it, Pratibha? I mean, winning for the fourth time in a row? You must have been born lucky."
"Nobody is born lucky. You have to be determined and hard working, that's all," replied Pratibha. "Come on, let's get a window seat in the bus."
"Where do you think they are taking us? I hope it's to Ajanta – I've never seen those caves, have you?"
"Ajanta's too far for a day trip, nearly 64 km to the south, one way. I think we'll do just about half that distance, perhaps to Yaval Wildlife Sanctuary in the north. Good thing I'm carrying my camera." The two friends jogged to the college gate, their sneakers leaving marks on the wet ground.

Little did the city of Jalgaon know that, in years to come, Pratibha Patil would leave her mark on its soil in more ways than one. For the time being, it continued to exist as before – a productive, agricultural region on the northern Deccan Plateau and an important collection and distribution centre of agricultural goods. Thanks to its rich volcanic soil, watered by the Tapti river, plenty of cotton and millet is produced here. It also has a large number of cotton-textile and vegetable-oil mills. You could also have your fill of tea, gold and bananas, which are in abundance. In fact, Jalgaon grows more bananas than any other district in the country!

Well-connected by rail and the national highway to Mumbai and Kolkata, Jalgaon has an interesting historic past. It used to be part of the territory controlled by the Holkar family of Maratha rulers. In 1818 Jalgaon became part of British India and in 1947 it came under independent India.

The girls of Moolji Jaitha College were thoroughly familiar with the history of their town, but right now it was geography which was their concern. Where were they headed for- Ajanta or Yaval? The bus driver pressed the horn loudly as a horde of excited and eager young women scrambled noisily into the bus.

3

The Call of Duty

As a woman I have no country. As a woman my country is the whole world.

—Virginia Woolf

3

"*H*ukum, please..."

She came to with a start, the tea-cup slipping ever so slightly in the saucer. The tea had finished long ago, but she had dozed off, into the world of her past within a matter of minutes. The routine pressures of administering a state usually left her too exhausted to sink into sentimental thoughts about family, and it was a luxury that she seldom allowed herself. There was, of course, the image of a practical, level-headed administrator to be kept up in office; besides, as a person she was very disciplined and focused, qualities that she expected her staff to emulate.

There was a hint of annoyance in her eyes as she looked up at the old and graying bearer who always served her at Mount Abu. Despite her instructions, he had not stopped calling her '*hukum*', a term that to her reeked of submission. While she appreciated the need for a pecking order, she felt there were some terms that had outlived their purpose.

Handing over the cup and saucer, she kicked off her flat-heeled sandals and arose from the chair to take a little stroll in the lawns of her official residence. Somehow she liked the lawns of the Mount Abu residence better than of the Raj Bhawan in Jaipur.The green springy grass felt cool under her bare feet and as she walked she felt some of the accumulated fatigue of the past few days slip away. This two day trip to Mount Abu was one of those rare indulgences she permitted herself as she really had felt she needed to get away from the searing heat of Jaipur and the pressing engagements of governorship and take a break.

The past week in Jaipur had been unusually hectic. In addition to the daily numerous appointments and meetings, attending to correspondence and official files, there had been a one-day whirlwind tour. Starting from Jaipur at six in the morning the short trip to Alwar had seemed much longer, on account of the endless potholes, particularly in the last stretch. If it could make her bones rattle in the cushioned, sturdy Scorpio, what did it do to the common man? She had immediately instructed her aide-de-camp to take up the matter of repair of this road with the office of the Chief Minister. Without good roads, how could they expect development to ever reach the people living in the villages?

As her eyes ran over the dry expanse from the window of her vehicle speeding towards Alwar, she thought of her home state, Maharashtra. What a contrast the two states were – in sight, smell and colour! Though somewhat similar in size, Maharashtra being the third largest state and Rajasthan the largest in India, they were quite different geographically. Maharashtra had the advantage of the Western Ghats, a hilly range running parallel to the coast, to the west of which lay the Konkan coastal plains, and to the east the flat Deccan Plateau. The state thus had no dearth of water, the Western Ghats forming one of the three watersheds of India, from which many South Indian rivers originated. To the north of the state, near the Madhya Pradesh border, lay the Satpura Range, lending a rich spread of green all around. She missed the smell of the humus-rich, black basalt or black soil of the Decaan Plateau and the endless fields of tall sugarcane.

Most of Rajasthan, in contrast, comprised the large, inhospitable Great Indian or Thar Desert, sandy and dry. Around it grew the northwestern thorn scrub forests in a band, between the desert and the Aravallis, receiving less than 400 mm of rain in an average year. Temperatures could rise even beyond 45°C in summer and drop below freezing point in the winter.

In the last three years as her bones had adjusted to the extreme changes in temperature, Pratibha had also learned to get used to and understand a little of Rajasthani, the mother tongue of the people of the state she was governing. Quite different from Marathi, in tone and tenor!

She liked the colourful sight of turbans, although they were much larger than the ones worn by Maharashtrian men and were also tied in a different manner. The bright ghaghra-choli and odhni of the Rajashtani women lent a burst of colour to an otherwise dull landscape, but Pratibha still yearned sometimes for a glimpse of the Maharashtrian sari, tied in such a special, perfect way.

The folk culture and music of both states, however, was equally vibrant and active. Festivals were celebrated with great enthusiasm, with everyone taking part in the making of delicious sweets and savouries and decorating their homes and towns.

Most of all, it was the spark in the youth - the enthusiasm and hope in the eyes of young students - that made her forget the rough ride and potholes on the way.

In Alwar it had been heartening to see the progress of the Gauri Devi Girls Primary School, the foundation stone of which she had laid just a year ago. Beautifully turned out in all their finery for their annual function, they had saluted her smartly and gracefully escorted her to her place of honour as Chief Guest. No matter what her commitments, she never missed a chance to encourage young girls, who she believed needed all the boost they could get. It was a long time, she felt, before would people realize the true meaning of the saying: "the hand that rocks the cradle rules the world."

After attending the function, she had driven to Sariska to review the progress of the Integrated Women's Community Centre. Started with the aim of enabling women to be economically independent, the Centre provided training to women in a number of vocations, ranging from block printing, tie and dye to tailoring of dresses. The unique feature was that it allowed women to choose a time and hour of their convenience between nine in the morning and six in the evening. This made it possible for young, unmarried girls, as well as middle-aged housewives, mothers and older women to benefit from it. It was a cause dear to her heart and no discomfort could keep her away from it. It was for this very reason that she had started a hostel for working women in Mumbai and the Industrial Training Institute for the blind in Jalgaon, her home town.

With that job done, the next halt was the District Commissioner's office, the agenda being the review of the computerization of land records which the administration had started. A quick, light lunch there, then back to Jaipur. En route, there was yet another stop at Dausa, a small town just east of

Jaipur, to preside over an award-giving function for the Best Entrepreneur of the Year, instituted by the local chamber of commerce.

Finally, they were nearing Jaipur. Despite her tiredness and preoccupation with various matters of state, the sight of Amber fort (Amer), 11 kilometres from the pink city, always lifted her spirits. In her three years as Governor, she had passed this way ever so often, but never found the time to go up. One day she would, she promised herself.

Once the citadel of the ruling Kachhawa clan of Amber, before Jaipur became the capital, the Amber Fort stood majestically amidst picturesque and rugged hills. Beautifully harmonising Hindu and Mughal architecture, and built in red sandstone and white marble, the fort had been constructed by Raja Man Singh in 1600 AD and completed by Sawai Jai Singh I in the eighteenth century. Belying its somewhat forbidding exterior, the inside is a paradise of a romantic palace, the interior walls depicting expressive scenes with paintings, carvings, precious stones and mirror settings.

Although she had visited it many years ago, as part of a college trip, time had not dimmed the details in her memory. They had gone up to the fort on elephant back, she and her friends, screeching in delight and fright as the heavy animal rocked them from side to side. Just as time had rocked, gently at first, from her cradle, to where she stood now.

4

The Early Days

There are only two lasting bequests we can hope to give our children. One is roots; the other, wings.

—Hodding Carter

4

While Jalgaon was where Pratibha Patil spent her formative years, her birthplace was Nadgaon. She was born on 19 December 1934 to Narayan Paglu Rao, a Maratha. Also known as Nanasaheb, and a member of the local administration board, Pratibha's father, unlike most male parents at that time, was proud to have been blessed with a daughter. "I shall make sure that she has the best education," he thought to himself, "I know she will go far in life." There must have been an inkling of things to come, for Narayan Paglu Rao was known to be an expert in the subject of astrology.

His decision to send his only daughter amongst six children to study in R.R. School, Jalgaon however, must have created quite a stir in the rest of the family, as in those days girls were supposed to stay at home and learn domstic skills, get married, have children, grandchildren...

Growing up in a traditional Maratha household, Pratibha had the good fortune to see, learn and adopt what she wished of her conservative family and at the same imbibe what modern education had to offer. Like most young girls, she loved pottering about in the kitchen, memorizing recipes by watching and analyzing the appetizing smells of different dishes. Festivals were particularly exciting, when sweets and specialties made her mouth water. She and her brother would slyly follow the servants carrying the baskets of sweets from the kitchen to other rooms, grabbing a handful and racing to the terrace before anyone could catch them.

In addition to the pleasures of forbidden fruit, or rather, sweets, Pratibha loved dressing up in traditional Indian clothes. The Maharashtrian sari was a favourite, while the soft, smooth silks, the dupattas with *gota* (golden lace borders), with jewellery and slippers to match, she felt, transformed her into a princess! Others must have thought so too, for she was chosen College Queen in 1962.

The young girl's physical growth was well complemented by her mind's insatiable quest for learning. After she completed her M.A. from Moolji Jaitha College, Jalgaon, she moved to Mumbai to study law at Government Law College, Mumbai, one of the oldest and most distinguished colleges in the country.

The establishment of the Government Law College was an intellectual breakthrough in itself, because prior to 1855, there was no formal legal education in British ruled India. The only source of such knowledge were the informal classes held after court hours by the then Chief Justice of the Supreme Court of Bombay, Sir Erskine Perry, for a small, select group of people. As the need for this discipline grew, conscious efforts were made to collect funds and institute a chair – the Perry Professorship of Jurisprudence – at the Elphinstone Institute. In 1855, the Government Law School or GLS (which later came to be known as Government Law College in 1925) was established and Dr. R.T. Reid, L.L.B, became its first Perry Professor.

Up to 1924, there were no women on the rolls of Government Law School for they were disqualified from enrolment as legal practitioners in India. The first woman to break through this male bastion was Cornelia Sorabjee, who succeeded in getting special permission from the University Senate to sit for the examination. Women were finally freed from this gender bias when a resolution was moved in their favour by Dr. Harisingh Gour in the Legislative Assembly on February 1, 1922.

It was here in Government Law College that Pratibha formed one of the best friendships of her life, with Usha Bhowmik, a co-student, who herself went on to become a lawyer, social worker and political activist. As Bhowmik states, "Pratibha was 28 years old then and already an MLA. Our friendship blossomed when she was appointed president of Bhartiya Grameen Mahila Sangh and I became the secretary in 1967." So close were they that when Usha's husband passed away in 1999, she used a shawl that Pratibha had gifted her, as a shroud.

Their friendship has withstood the test and travails of time, and it was Usha who was fortunate to be the first to share Pratibha's most important moment of her political career. Bhowmik was with Patil when she received the first message from New Delhi regarding her nomination for President in early June. "I had gone to visit her in Jaipur. We were returning in the salon train from Mount Abu when the message came. I had retired to my room but she sent her maid to call me so that she could share the news with me," says Usha, who was with Patil from May 29 to June 17, 2007 in Rajasthan. Usha reveals an interesting aspect of Pratibha's character, "Pratibha is very persistent, diligent and consistent. Once she decides she likes you, she is fiercely loyal to you. No one can sway her."

Despite the heavy academic demands of the law course at Government Law College, Pratibha still found time to pursue her passion for sports. As in Jalgaon, in GLC too she was an active participant in inter-college tournaments, winning shields in table-tennis. By this time she had become used to ascending the victory stand, but now it was time for her to share another, very special platform, with her match partner in life.

5

A Lasting Partnership

The goal in marriage is not to think alike, but to think together.

—Robert C. Dodds

5

In the 1960s, the average acceptable age for a woman to marry was eighteen to nineteen years. For women of progressive and educated families, it could go up to the early or mid-twenties. But by any standards, thirty and above was rather late, raising many an eyebrow from friends and relatives alike. Also, giving and accepting dowry was the norm in most families, regardless of their socio-economic status.

As far as Pratibha's father's was concerned, dowry was not an issue, because by the time she made up her mind to contest her first election in 1962, he had told his daughter, "I have some money put aside for you. But I have decided I am not paying your dowry. If you want to contest the elections, you will need money. So you can use this egg nest I have collected for you for your politics."

Pratibha was of the same view anyway and replied firmly, "I will not marry a man who wants money from my father." Perhaps that is why she had to wait long, till 31 years of age, before she met the right man, Devisingh Ramsingh Shekhawat, a Rajput, and married him on 7 July 1965. They were well suited because he too did not want to marry for money and wanted an educated wife.

Devisingh, also a Maharashtrian, was an educator by profession, whose family had moved from the Shekhawati region of Rajasthan to Jalgaon a few generations back. He was a former mayor of Amravati, a city in Maharashtra, believed to be the city of Lord Indra. Amravati has interesting legends of romance and patriotism linked to it. The story goes that when Lord Krishna took Rukmini away from her wedding ceremony, they escaped through a tunnel from the Amba Devi temple in Amravati to Koundynapur, another spiritual place. Although the tunnel still exists, it is closed. It is also said that when freedom fighter Bhagat Singh went underground, he hid in Amravati for three days.

In a way both husband and wife – Devisingh and Pratibha – hailed from places that strongly promoted the sporting spirit. While Pratibha had been encouraged all along to excel in sports during school and college, Devisingh's hometown, Amravati, boasted of the famous physical education institution called the Hanuman Vyayam Prasarak Mandal or HVPM. Founded by late Dr. Shivajirao Patwardhan in 1928, the institute provides training to students from all over the country in a number of sports, including taekwondo. It is well equipped with two large running tracks, a stadium, an international-level swimming pool and two indoor stadiums.

Although Devisingh and Pratibha were now treading a common track in life, they chose to pursue their own individual interests, but all the while supporting each other. Interestingly, while the Rajput bahu retained the *pallu* over her head, she chose to keep her maiden surname – Patil. Though this is a trend that is growing today but nearly half a century ago it must have caused a stir. In fact, most married women today prefer to retain their maiden name in the middle and the husband's surname last; Pratibha, all those years ago, did the reverse choosing to call herself Pratibha Devisingh Patil. Pratibha's younger brother, Dr. G.N. Patil, explains her decision thus, "At the time of her marriage, she was popular as Pratibha Patil. By then she had already created a political identity for herself. She didn't want to lose her identity. So she continued to call herself Patil instead of Shekhawat."

Right at the start of their married life, Devisingh assured his wife that he would never stand in the way of her political ambitions and career. He proved to be a pillar of strength throughout but kept away from state politics himself. When Pratibha became the first and only woman minister in Maharashtra in the V.P. Naik cabinet, he even moved to Mumbai (then Bombay) for her sake, as she was hesitant to live alone in the ministerial bungalow allotted to her.

Although they have spent most of their time apart, they share several common interests. Together, they have established Vidya Bharati Shikshan Prasarak Mandal, which runs a chain of schools and colleges in Jalgaon and Mumbai. All in all, Devisingh is very proud of his wife's political progress. As he states, "I have sacrificed so much...it has been worth it".

Apart from her husband, Pratibha received tremendous support from her extended family even after marriage. Thanks to her two widowed aunts (mother's sisters), who looked after her home and children right through their schooldays, she was able to be a working mother without the accompanying pressures. When her son, Rajendra, and daughter Jyoti became older, Devisingh shifted them to Amravati for higher education.

Whether away from family or together with them, Pratibha has performed the role of wife, mother and grandmother as sincerely as her political duties. It a well-known fact that the way to a man's heart is through his stomach, and Pratibha Patil is believed to be a very good cook. As someone put it, she "hates lies and loves curry", her own favourites being rice, ghee, and curd curry! Whenever she is with the family, it is she who turns out mouth-watering dishes from the kitchen.

Pratibha's brother, Dr G.N. Patil, recalls an interesting incident. "Once we - tai, me and our maternal aunt - were going to Sindkheda, a village in Dhule district, to visit our maternal uncle's house. We were not more than six years old at that time. Those days, one had to cross a river to reach Sindkheda. We were carrying our lunch with us, which included rice, dal and curry. As soon as we left home, tai opened the tiffin box and quickly gobbled up all the curry." He says that after that she was so desperate for more curry that she refused to cross the river until she got it. Finally, their maternal aunt told her that if she crossed the river it would automatically turn into curry. Pratibha actually believed her and crossed the river!

Rajendra, Pratibha's son remembers how, as children, he and his sister resented their mother's attention being shared by so many others, but she always said that her doors would be open for everyone. Her granddaughters, adore her and as Nilima Patil puts it, "Whenever she comes, she is a grandmother and not a politician. She is the idol for me and all other girls."

6

Pratibha Tai

We have learned that power is a positive force if it is used for positive purposes.

—Elizabeth Dole

6

Pratibha Patil's grandchildren are not the only ones who idolize her. The people of the village Nadgaon adore her so much that they call her Mukta Tai Ma, after the local goddess. According to Pratibha's classmate, Venkatesh Phadnis, a retired journalist, "People keep her picture in their home and pray to her because of all that she's done for them."

He is not alone in his observation. There are several people who have received her help and generosity, and as a result of which they stand proud on their feet today. One of them is 35-year old Prafullata More, who lost the ability to walk because of a road accident eight years ago. Soon after Prafullata also lost her parents. Rendered homeless and helpless, her relatives took turns to shelter her for a while, but then abandoned her at a temple near Kalanagar.

It was at this point that the Shrama Sadhana Trust Hostel, Bandra took her in, providing free accommodation and food. For Prafullata, "It's like a home and it's all thanks to Pratibha Patil." The past four years have been a "peaceful life" for Prafullata, who works at a temple office near the hostel.

The Shrama Sadhana Trust Hostel for working women was founded by Pratibha Patil in 1978. It is managed by her son, Rajendra Shekhawat, and has a capacity of 103 rooms, which can accommodate 250 working women. Dhyaneshwar Patil, who has been working with the hostel as an accountant for the past thirteen years, reveals that Pratibha is very particular about keeping the fees at a level that working women from lower middle and middle class families can afford. Although the hostel has spacious rooms and is housed in a prime location, the fee for a room for two is a reasonable Rs.2,000 per month. Similar hostels are run by the Trust in Pune and Delhi, benefiting people from all walks of life – software engineers, surgeons, assistant commissioner of police...

Pratibha has touched the lives of young and old alike. The elders of Bodhwad taluka, Nadgaon, Pratibha's birthplace, call her 'beti'. They too have their tales of gratitude. A smile writ all over her wrinkled face, Sarjabai relates emotionally, "Taisaheb gave my out-of-work grandson a job in her college. Who am I? Just a neighbour. But for me she is a sister."

Ganesh Guruji is eager to narrate his experience. "She got the roof of the Ram temple repaired by donating Rs.1,00,000," he says.

Be it neighbours or family, Pratibha is known to give sound, practical advice. Her nephew, Virendrasingh Patil recalls, "When I became the Panchayat Samiti chairman, I wanted a car." But his aunt's matter-of-fact suggestion was, "Don't buy a car as you will get into wrong means to meet petrol expenses. Just use a two-wheeler." He is thankful that he heeded her words, because of which he has a clean image today.

Yet another recipient of her good wishes is orthopaedic surgeon Dr. Ghanshyam Kochure in Jalgaon, son of a resthouse guard, Gendulal Yashwant Kochure. Belonging to the Mahar community, Dr. Kochure's father realized that his son, the second amongst eight children, despite scoring well in school, could not progress much in Nadgaon, so he took a transfer to Jalgaon, where there were good colleges.

Dr. Kochure reminisces, "I have known Pratibha tai since I was five years old...whatever I have achieved in life is because of her. She noticed a brilliance in me as a child and told my father that he must encourage me to study further...if my father needed any kind of assistance, then she was ready to help him." Today Dr. Kochure runs a 30-bed hospital in Jalgaon and does not charge a fee from patients who cannot afford it.

Following his example, Dr. Kochure's brothers too showed serious interest in their studies and are well settled in life. Professor Vinod Kochure teaches at a college in Bhusawal. He says, "Our entire family is indebted to Pratibha tai. She changed the lives of the children of a watchman...never discriminated against us...all of us brothers practise her philosophy of life, to do good for humanity."

Social work has been part and parcel of Pratibha's activities, at an individual as well as political level, from the time she was in her twenties. Her entry into politics merely provided her a larger and more effective platform for implementing her ideas especially those regarding the welfare of women and children.

7

Entry Into Politics

Ideas are great arrows, but there has to be a bow. And politics is the bow of idealism.

—Bill Moyers

7

Politics for Pratibha was familiar ground, and definitely something she had inherited from her father. Father and daughter shared more than a few traits and interests. He was an advocate; she practised law in the Jalgaon court after completing her L.L.B. Narayanrao was already involved in the local politics; Pratibha's first step into this sphere happened to be a matter of chance.

In 1957, Pratibha had participated in the Maharashtra Assembly election campaign to help her mentor and Principal, Y.S. Mahajan, who was a candidate fielded by the Congress. She organized groups of volunteers and distributed pamphlets to appeal for votes, thus contributing to Mahajan's winning the election by a huge margin. This kindled her interest in politics and also boosted her own confidence and was probably a major factor which spurred her entry into politics.

In 1960 Pratibha gave a fiery speech at the Akhil Bharatiya Rajput Parishad, after which her father encouraged her to enter the political arena. There was no turning back after that. She became a full-fledged political figure at the young age of twenty-seven, winning the 1962 Maharashtra Assembly election as a candidate from the Jalgaon constituency. From 1962 to 1985 she was a member of the Maharashtra Assembly and never lost an election that she contested. During this period she was a minister holding varied portfolios – urban development and housing, education, tourism, parliamentary affairs, public health and social welfare, cultural affairs – rising from the rank of deputy minister to cabinet minister for state.

In the initial years her guiding light was ex-Chief Minister and senior Congress leader Yashwantrao Chavan. Under his watchful eye, Pratibha became a deputy minister for education in the Vasantrao Naik ministry after being re-elected in 1967. In her following terms, from 1972 to 1978, she enjoyed the position of full cabinet minister for state.

Walking down memory lane, Wincy Chacko, an old colleague recalls the early days of Pratibha's political career. "During my 15-year vice presidentship of Mahila Congress Bombay Regional Committee, Pratibha was the MPCC president...we had shared several forums. She was a soft-spoken, small-built woman. Her speeches were not fire-spitting, but temperate and meaningful."

In the wake of current developments, Wincy, a

former active Congress worker herself, adds, "She has proven her administrative capabilities. She will be a wonderful President. A gem of a woman who will outperform many of her predecessors."

However, it was not smooth sailing all the way. The 1970s were turbulent times for the country and the ruling Congress government in particular. Many tough decisions had to be taken, and even seasoned politicians were in two minds as to which way they should go. Ventakesh Phadnis recalls the time when Patil met Indira Gandhi. It was 1970, and Jalgaon was engulfed in riots. At a packed rally, Indira Gandhi announced that she was depending on Pratibha, then a deputy minister in the Maharashtra government, to restore normalcy in Jalgaon.

The close of the year 1977 was a time for testing loyalties. Following the Emergency (1975-1977) and Indira Gandhi's defeat, there was a split in the Congress. Senior leaders of the state Congress (I), such as Sharad Pawar as well as many juniors joined the Congress (Urs) party formed by Devraj Urs. When Sharad Pawar, as head of the Purogami Lok Dal, became Chief Minister of Maharashtra for the first time in July 1979, Pratibha Patil stood steadfast with the Congress, and became leader of the Opposition after forming an alliance with the Jan Sangh. This act of loyalty was remembered and much appreciated by Rajiv Gandhi and later, Sonia Gandhi.

53

Ironically, on the very date that tai (as Pratibha is popularly called) was born – December 19 – of the year 1977, the then Prime Minister Indira Gandhi was put under arrest during the Janata Party rule. While many a 'loyal' changed colour and switched sides in that crucial time, Pratibha refused to celebrate. Marching to the Collector's office, she demanded, "You have to arrest me too. If Mrs Gandhi goes in, so do I."
Rama Rao, the Collector, tried to reason with her, "Listen, Pratibha, you don't know what you are saying. Don't be emotional. I tell you what – I will record your arrest on paper, but you can quietly go home. Be sensible."
"You mean you want me to lie? No way. And I don't want bail either. I shall go to jail."

And she did. Ten days later, after Mrs Gandhi was released from prison, Pratibha too came out from behind the bars. Thus was forged a lasting bond between the Gandhi family and Pratibha Patil, who served them in many ways in times of difficulty and even managed the kitchen in Indira Gandhi's home after Sanjay Gandhi's death.

In 1981, when the Congress (I) regained power, Pratibha's name was considered for the Chief Ministership of Maharashtra, but the post went to A.R. Antulay, a confidant of Sanjay Gandhi. However, Antulay had to resign within a very short period, on account of charges of corruption. Subsequently, Pratibha became a minister in the Vasantdada Patil ministry.

In 1985 she was elected to the Rajya Sabha and in the very next year in 1986 she crossed yet another milestone, ascending to the position of deputy chairperson of the Rajya Sabha, where she remained from November 18, 1986 to November 5, 1988. During these two years she also headed the Parliamentary Committee on privileges.

There were major differences between her and the then Maharashtra Pradesh Congress Committee (MPCC) chief, Prabhu Rao. Taking stock of the situation, Rajiv Gandhi appointed her as MPCC chief (1988-1990).

In 1990 her Rajya Sabha term expired. In 1991 Pratibha won the 10th Lok Sabha elections on a Congress ticket from her husband's city, Amravati, of which he had once been mayor. And it was from here that Pratibha Patil climbed the political ladder, from an enthusiastic campaigner to the national parliament in the 10th Lok Sabha.

This lady, who had never lost an election in a span of thirty-four years, had more or less decided to spend the evening of her political life in quiet retirement after the end of her tenure in the Lok Sabha in 1996. She would be politically visible only as a participant in the party's campaign in elections in Maharashtra.

But, even without politics, there was plenty to keep her occupied in the sphere of social welfare.

Her family was running as many as eighteen educational institutions including schools, colleges and technical training institutions. Back in 1974, she had started the Pratibha Mahila Sahakari Bank for women and promoted the concept of working women's hostels. Another issue close to her heart was the welfare and prosperity of farmers, to realize which, she and some others had set up the Sant Muktabai Sahakari Sakhar Karkhana Ltd. in Jalgaon.

However, destiny had something else in store.

In November 2004 the Congress leadership roused her from her political hibernation and appointed her as Governor of Rajasthan. Thus in 2004 Rajasthan got its first woman Governer. After Vasantdada Patil, she was the second politician from Maharashtra in this post. Interestingly, her governorship added to an already women-empowered administration in the state, with Vasundhara Raje as Chief Minister and Sumitra Singh Assembly Speaker.

It was the beginning of an era of higher political prestige, and a sign of bigger things to come.

8

The Governor of Rajasthan

*Genuine politics – even politics worthy of the name–
the only politics I am willing to devote myself to is
simply a matter of serving those around us: serving
the community and serving those who will come after
us. Its deepest roots are moral because it is a responsibility expressed through action, to and for the whole.*

—Vaclav Havel

8

All through her political life, Pratibha Patil was non-controversial, unassuming and media shy, but as Governor of Rajasthan she revealed a little-known facet of her personality. She proved to be a stickler for taking constitutionally correct decisions even at the risk of being politically unpopular and not yielding to the pressure of either the opposition or her own political party.

She ruffled many feathers when as Governor, she returned, unsigned, the Rajasthan Religious Freedom Bill 2006, originally the Raj Dharma Swatantrya Bill, 2006 passed by the Rajasthan Legislative Assembly on 7 April 2006. The Rajasthan government had introduced the Bill alleging that "some religious and other institutions, bodies and individuals are involved in unlawful conversion from one religion to another by allurement or by fraudulent means or forcibly."

In India, a Governor, who is the nominal head of a state government, in order to ensure that the

Constitutional provisions are upheld, almost never refuses to sign a Bill passed by the Assembly. Governor Pratibha Patil refused to sign it because she found that some of its provisions infringed upon the fundamental rights of freedom of speech and expression and freedom to profess, practise and propagate religion. She suggested that representatives refer it to the President of India for passage if they so desired. Under Article 200 of the Indian Constitution, the President can sign Bills into law if a state Governor refuses to do so.

Rajasthan's then law minister, Ghanshyam Tiwari, was quoted as reacting thus to her action, "It was the constitutional obligation of the Governor to sign the Bill that was passed by the legislative assembly." He added that the Bill would be sent back to the Governor if it received cabinet approval. Social Welfare Minister Madan Dilawar felt, "... We are stuck. The Rajasthan society is suffering because of her refusal."

On the other hand, Christian organizations such as the All India Christian Council (AICC) and the Christian Legal Association of India, and human rights organizations like the People's Union of Civil Liberties, were satisfied with the stand taken by the Governor. According to them, under the proposed anti-conversion law, it would become extremely easy for Hindu fundamentalists to lodge false accusations against Christian workers. The Bill provided for the immediate arrest of the accused even before any investigation was conducted.

They were of the view that the Bill treated conversion from Hinduism to Christianity differently than conversion from Christianity to Hinduism, thereby violating Article 14 of the Constitution, which promises equality before the law.

The Bill explicitly exempted "reconversion" of Christian converts to Hinduism from its purview by defining conversion as adopting a religion other than that of one's forefathers.

These organizations also warned that the legislation could give Hindu fundamentalists a chance to term any social work among people of other faiths as "allurement" – loosely defined as "offer of any temptation in the form of any gift or gratification, either in cash or kind or grant of any material benefit, either monetary or otherwise."

In its definition of "force," the Bill included "threat of divine displeasure", which could be used to ban any Christian literature speaking about heaven and hell and the consequences of sin and rejecting Christ's claims.

The Bill also sought identical punishment for those convicted of converting by the use of fraud, allurement or force as for those "attempting to convert", whereas in all other Indian laws the punishment for attempted crimes was less than that of executing them.

Enos Das Pradhan, general secretary of the National Council of Churches in India, denounced the Bill as "an instrument to harass the Christians." Counteracting these charges, Rajasthan lawmakers claimed that the Bill was intended to maintain religious harmony and civil order in the state.

Governor Patil's stand on the Bill was upheld by Dr John Dayal, secretary general of the All India Christian Council (AICC), in these words, "We are thankful to Governor Pratibha Patil for paying heed to the nationwide outcry, not only in the Christian community but also in the entire secular polity, against the Bill whose intention and nefarious motives were nothing less than to divide the people on religious lines and injure the secular polity of the state and the nation. This is a triumph of the democratic and secular values enshrined in our Constitution – for which our nation is known in the world."

The legislation also attracted the interest of Pope Benedict XVI, who conveyed to India's new ambassador to the Vatican, Amitava Tripathi, that the country should "firmly reject" attempts "to legislate clearly discriminatory restrictions on the fundamental right to religious freedom." The Pope had also taken note of the "disturbing signs of religious intolerance which had troubled some regions of the nation."

Professor Rajiv Gupta, a sociologist in Rajasthan University, was of the view that, "If she had passed the Anti-Conversion Bill, Rajasthan would have been plunged into an era of communal hatred. Pratibha Patil was aware of this grave threat. That's why she refused the Bill and played the role of a Constitutional protector."

In May 2006 the Bill was re-sent to Pratibha Patil, noting that similar anti-conversion laws had been enacted by Congress governors in Madhya Pradesh and Orissa forty years ago and upheld by the Supreme Court. A similar bill, the Himachal Pradesh Freedom of Religion Act 2006, passed later was promptly signed by the governor of the state. When drafting Article 25 of the Constitution, the head of the Constituent Assembly, Dr B.R. Ambedkar had said that it would be better to leave it to the state legislatures to make laws for regulating conversions. Governor Pratibha Patil took one year to send the Bill to Dr Kalam, the then President of India – a day before resigning as Governor on 21 June 2007. The irony of the situation is that finally she will have to take a decision on this Bill in her capacity as President.

Another glimpse of the non-partisan nature of erstwhile Governor Patil was provided during the Gujjar agitation in May 2007 in which twenty-five people lost their lives in the violence over the Gujjar demand for tribal status. Keen to embarrass the Raje government, the Congress demanded President's rule in the state. However, although Ms Patil spoke firmly to Vasundhara Raje in private, she refused to bow to pressure from the Congress. In the words of Justice Pana Chand Jain, a retired Judge of the Rajasthan High Court, "She displayed political maturity and advised Chief Minister Raje to tackle the law and order situation more effectively. Patil played her constitutional role with finesse." As someone commented she "has proved to be a cool lady in the hot seat."

Evidently a person unafraid of taking clear decisions, Ms Patil was very popular among her staff, who described her as "polite and gentle". As one member of the staff stated, "She always kept herself well-informed and read widely on economic reforms and education." A perfectionist at work, he also said that she would insist on her speeches being prepared after detailed study. And often, she would make several changes in them.

A woman with the human touch, the Raj Bhavan staff recalls the times she went out of her way to help them. Assistant Public Relations Officer at the Raj Bhavan Lokesh Sharma mentioned that when the washerman at the Governor's residence lost his elder son, Ms Patil visited his house. She provided financial help and also asked him to take Voluntary Retirement, thereafter giving his job to his daughter-in-law.

Quietly and steadily, the erstwhile governor of Rajasthan worked in a committed manner for the education of the rural poor. Her view is that, "Economically our country is progressing. But economic disparities are growing. We need to rectify this."

An issue that has always been close to Pratibha Patil's heart is empowerment of women. In Raj Bhavan, her door had always been open for the groups championing the cause of women's empowerment. She had taken active interest in pursuing the welfare of war widows in Rajasthan, personally writing to them and following the developments in each case. A sign of things to come? After all, as President of the country, she would assume the responsibility of supreme commander of the armed forces.

9

The President's Chair

All the world is a stage,
And all the men and women merely players.
They have their exits and entrances;
Each man in his time plays many parts.

—Shakespeare

9

The President's chair is the most prestigious po sition in the country, and Rashtrapati Bhavan – the 340-room palace on Raisina Hill, larger than Louis XIV's Versailles - the most eminent address. To achieve the status of first citizen, a person has to be of high personal integrity and an untainted past.

The first woman to try her luck to get into the Rashtrapati Bhavan, Manhohara Holkar, was a Maharashtrian. One among eight candidates in the fourth presidential election in 1967, she could not secure a single vote. It was Dr Zakir Hussain who won and became the first Muslim president of India.

The second woman candidate for the Presidential post was Furcharan Kaur, who fared better. She took on V.V. Giri in 1969 and came out fifth among fifteen candidates. The number of votes she secured was 940, but V.V. Giri made it to the President's chair with 401,515 votes.

In 2002, the Left fielded freedom fighter Captain Lakshmi Sahgal, who got 107,366 votes against former President A.P.J. Kalam's whopping 922,884. So, the absence of a lady in Raisina Hill to date has not been for want of trying.

The question is: how did Pratibha Patil come into the running? Particularly at a time when she was more or less into political retirement? Most people had expected that Dr Kalam, with his impeccable record, stature and immense popularity with young and old alike would continue for another term, or that Vice-President Bhairon Singh Shekhawat might step into his shoes.

The ruling coalition government at the centre, the United Progressive Allliance (UPA), till the last moment, turned down one nominee after another. It refused to consider Home Minister Shivraj Patil after the furore regarding his links with Puttaparthi Sathya Sai Baba and objections raised by the Left. The UPA fielded seven to nine candidates for this position. When Shivraj Patil's name was removed from the list, Sonia Gandhi proposed a woman candidate. In fact, her shortlist included Mohsina Kidwai, Nirmala Deshpande and Pratibha Patil. The first, for whom Mrs Indira Gandhi had always had a soft corner, was rejected on account of being a Muslim, the same faith as the outgoing President. Deshpande was a Gandhian but that seemed insufficient. Thus the only person left was Pratibha, who seemed to have all the credentials – she was close to the Gandhi family whom she had supported in rough weather, was of the right caste (Leva Patil), and, was the Governor of Rajasthan.

The strange thing is that Sonia Gandhi made her choice known to Prime Minister Manmohan Singh as late as 14 June 2007, asserting that the country would be proud to have a woman President in its 60th year of independence. Although the reactions to Patil's name were mixed – ranging from Prakash Karat's not knowing "enough about her" to CPI A.B. Bardhan's description of her as "an outstanding choice", Pratibha Patil was declared a nominee before people even had time to blink.

As the time for reckoning drew near, there was a mixed feeling in the country. Would Raisina Hill really see a lady in the chair? Was she good enough for it? Would she uphold the honour of the Presidential post?

But what does it really take to be the President of India? To be nominated as a Presidential candidate, a person must be a citizen of India, of 35 years of age or above, a member of the Lok Sabha who does not hold any office of profit under the government. Exceptions to this last provision are: the current Vice-President, the Governor of any state, and a minister of the Union or of any state. Should any of such three be elected President, he would have to vacate his previous office on the date he begins serving the nation in the capacity of President.

It is the elected members of the Vidhan Sabha of each state, Lok Sabha and Rajya Sabha who elect the President. Votes are allocated in a manner that there is a balance between the population of each state and the number of votes that can be cast by Assembly members from a state. Besides, there must be an equal balance between State Assembly members and National Parliament members. If there is a situation where no candidate receives a majority of votes, there is a system to eliminate losing candidates from the contest and transfer votes for them to other candidates, until one gains a majority. The normal tenure for a President is five years, after which he can stand for re-election.

Although the President of India's role is, for the most part, ceremonial – the actual executive authority lying with the Council of Ministers headed by the Prime Minister – he does have significant powers. In fact, the powers of the President of India may well be compared with those of the monarch of the United Kingdom. Apart from being the head of state, the President is the Supreme Commander of the Indian armed forces. He enjoys the executive powers of appointing the Prime Minister and other members of the Council of Ministers, and of distributing their portfolios on the Prime Minister's advice. In addition, the President is responsible for appointing the Governors of states, the Chief Justice, Judges of the Supreme Court and High Courts, the Attorney-General, the Comptroller and Auditor General, the Chief Election Commissioner and other Election Commissioners, the Chairman and other Members of the Union Public Service Commission, as well as Ambassadors and High Commissioners to other countries.

The President of India also has the power, solely on his discretion, to grant pardon or reduce the sentence of a convicted person, particularly in cases where a death sentence has been passed.

Some of the legislative powers enjoyed by the President are summoning and proroguing of both Houses of Parliament, and even dissolving the Lok Sabha, albeit on the advice of the Council of Ministers headed by the Prime Minister. It is the President who inaugurates Parliament with his address after general elections as well as at the beginning of the first session each year. Bills passed by Parliament can become law only after receiving the President's assent.

The President has the power to declare three types of emergency: (a) National emergency, in a situation of war, external aggression or internal rebellion; (b) State emergency, or President's rule, in the event of failure of Constitutional machinery in a state; (c) Financial emergency, when the economic situation is such as to pose a threat to the financial stability or credit of the country.

Naturally, there are many who would aspire to rise to this stature but few who actually make it to the Rashtrapati Bhavan. This official residence of the first citizen, located at the west end of the two and a half kilometre-long Rajpath, was known as the Viceroy House when India was governed by the British. It was renamed Government House after the country gained independence. Finally, when India became a republic in 1952, it came to be known as Rashtrapati Bhavan or President's House.

Apart from its national and political significance, Rashtrapati Bhavan is an architectural delight. Combining the best of Mughal and classical European architectural styles, it has a huge copper dome on the top of a long colonnade. The entrance to the portico has 31 steps and 20 columns. The Durbar or audience hall, just across the portico, has imposing golden pillars and coloured marble from all parts of India, and an elegantly carved 2300-year-old sculpture of the Ashokan bull at the entrance. This is where all official functions of the President, including the National Award ceremonies, take place. Behind the President's chair stands a statue of Gautam Buddha from the 4th century. Not many people are aware that for a number of years the hall served as a museum until the present venue of the National Museum was constructed.

The rectangular Ashoka Hall, earlier known as the State Ball Room, is the venue for formal gatherings such as accepting credentials from foreign diplomats, swearing-in ceremonies of ministers, and the like. Decorated with several chandeliers, from its windows the hall offers a beautiful view of the Mughal Gardens. There is a guest room for the visiting dignitaries with two spacious suites furnished with teak furniture and beautifully woven Indian carpets. The State dining room or the Banquet Hall can seat 104 people. Its teak-panelled walls are adorned with full-size portraits of the former Presidents of India. In the Council room, where the formal conferences of the President are hosted, there are murals of sea routes to India done by Indian artists but conceived by the famous art historian Percy Brown. The Art Gallery and the Marble Hall are a treasure trove of various works of art – paintings, portraits and statues - collected over the years by the Viceroys and the Presidents of India.

Described as a masterpiece of symmetry, discipline, silhouette and harmony, Rashtrapati Bhavan on Raisina Hill is a majestical classical structure. Designed by Edwin Lutyens, the world-famous architect, its construction began in 1913. The work was completed in eight years by over 3,500 men working on 3.5 million cubic feet of marble. As many as 1,700 million bricks were used! The total area covered by this palatial residence is 18,580 sq metres or 200,000 sq ft. The cost, back then, was a whopping Rs.1.4 million. The first person to occupy this august residence was Viceroy Lord Irwin, who stepped into it on 23 January 1931.

From then to now, it has been a long journey indeed, and the beginning of a new era, as the first woman President of India makes her way through Gate 35 to the President's chair.

10

Celebration Time

We don't accomplish anything in this world alone...and whatever hapens is the result of the whole tapestry of one's life and all the weavings of individual threads from one to another that creates something.

—Sandra Day O'Connor

10

The sleepy little village of Chhoti Losal in Rajasthan was in a festive mood. Its prediction that its daughter-in-law, Pratibha Devisingh Patil, "is going to win hands down" in the thirteenth Presidential election had come true. The *bahu* had made sure that this village of barely 4000 people, with a dominant population of Rajputs, would mark its presence on the political map of the world down the ages. The women sang a special song written for the ocasion, 'Dadi baniya Rashtrapati.' and danced through the lanes, celebrating a second Holi in celebration. Men, women and children alike were all preparing to attend her inaugural ceremony in New Delhi, to make it the most colourful ever.

Although Patil had not been as frequent a visitor to Chhoti Losal as her rival Bhairon Singh Shekhawat had to his home town, the people regarded her as *'dadi maan sa'* or grandma. And whenever she did go, she made it a point to meet everyone in the village. The temple bells of Chhoti

Losal had been ringing ever since news of her filing her nomination. 'Karanimata' being the family deity of the Shekhawat families, a recital of the Durga 'sahastranam' for 4-6 hours a day had begun at the Karanimata Temple, with an 'akhandjot' being lit before the goddess till the results were declared.

The family *haveli* was built by Pratibha's grand-father-in-law, Jagat Singh Shekhawat, who had migrated to Amravati a century ago but kept returning to Chhoti Losal. It is now inhabited by Sukh Ram Shekhawat, Devisingh's cousin. There has been a stream of visitors to the haveli recently, most of the locals gathering in the shade of the banyan tree near it, now converted into a 'chaupal'. Another attraction was the television in the nearby shop, where news of the Presidential election was followed with great eagerness. And now the aspirations of the villagers had been fulfilled.

Describing her win as the victory of the principles upheld by the people of the country, the new President said, "I am grateful to the voters. I am grateful to the people of India, the men and women of India," soon after she defeated Opposition-backed independent candidate Bhairon Singh Shekhawat with a big margin of over three lakh votes. In the final count, Patil got 6,38,116 votes while Shekhawat secured 3,31,306 in an electoral college of 10.98 lakh.

The counting of votes lasted six hours, at the end of which Lok Sabha Secretary-General and returning officer P.D.T. Achary announced that the winner got 65.82 per cent of the valid votes. In Parliament, it was Patil: 442 votes, Shekhawat: 232. In the states and union territories put together, she had a clear win of 2,489 votes against the loser's 1,217.

When she had been nominated, and before leaving Jaipur for New Delhi, she had thanked the state government and stated that her first job as President would be to make a success of the National Rural Employment Guarantee Act (NREGA), which had been started by the UPA. When queried about her priorities if she were elected President, she had replied, "I know India is doing great under the Prime Ministership of Dr Manmohan Singh. But still there are a few dark areas. For example, the poor — they must all be raised above the poverty line. We must put science and technology to good use to improve their lives. Women's empowerment is another issue. I would stress on rural development and agriculture too. We are making good economic progress but the benefits should filter down to the poor. There are also other areas which people pay little heed to. The social evils of female foeticide and child marriages. My stress has always been on women empowerment. Such empowerment cannot happen if these issues are not addressed."

As the time drew near for her to take the Presidential oath, she knew there was a long, hard road to tread. Promises to keep, and miles to go before sleep...

11

The Republic's First Servant

My will shall shape the future. Whether I fail or succeed shall be no man's doing but my own. I am the force; I can clear any obstacle before me or I can be lost in the maze. My choice; my responsibility; win or lose, only I hold the key to my destiny.

—Elaine Maxwell

11

July 25, 2007 dawned. The capital of India, cov
ered with grey but rainless clouds, was all set
to receive its first woman President in office. The
citizens of Delhi, cutting across barriers of age,
colour, caste and creed, sat glued to their television
sets to catch every moment of the solemn ceremony
that involved the handing over of charge by the
incumbent President, Dr. APJ Abdul Kalam to the
elected one.

At about one o'clock in the afternoon, all cam-
eras zoomed in on the pristine white house on
9, South Avenue, from where the President-elect,
Ms Pratibha Devisingh Patil, would be given a
formal, written invitation, as per protocol, by the
military secretary to the President, Major-General
Vinod Chopra, and escorted to Rashtrapati Bhavan
for the change of guard. As news reporters did a
runthrough of the personal and political life of sixty-
three years old Ms Patil, one could see a bunch
of people at a permissible distance from the house.
There was the former Chief Minister of Maharashtra,

and people from Jalgoan and Amravati. While a few were distant relatives and school friends of the first citizen-to-be, there were members of several educational institutions and co-operative banks, waiting eagerly but patiently for Ms Patil to emerge.

There was a shifting of people at the front door, and Ms Pratibha Patil came out in a white silk sari with a green border and full-sleeved blouse, *pallu* drawn over her head, a deep red round bindi on her forehead, the oval, plastic-framed spectacles perched on her nose, and a small purse in hand. With firm, unhurried steps, she walked to the Presidential car – an ebony-coloured Mercedes, which had an immaculately polished Ashok Chakra at the front and rear, and the *'tiranga'* in the front right. The Mercedes had taken over this coveted roled from the royal horse-driven carriage of by-gone days. Once Ms Patil and her husband, Devisingh Shekhawat were seated, the motorcade drove off without delay to Rashtrapati Bhavan.

There, without much ado, they were taken into the study of President APJ Abdul Kalam. After a short exchange of formalities, President Kalam, unassuming as usual, wearing a deep blue *band gala* suit, the silver-grey hair falling just short of both eyebrows, and the President-to-be came out to stand before the Presidential bodyguards for the national salute. Standing erect to the call of the bugle, sword pointing down, they looked resplendent in their white and red attire, astride their well-groomed horses. It was interesting to note that the standard *'shriman'* had been dropped from the words of the salute – someone had looked into the minutest detail! The Presidential bodyguards had actually been raised way back in the time of Governor General Warren Hastings. During war, their strength had even gone up to 2,000.

They had a significant role to play on this occasion. Salute over, Kalam and Patil smilingly exchanged notes, then stepped into the car for the short journey to Centrall Hall, Parliament House, the venue for the Presidential oath-taking ceremony. As per tradition, the bugler rode on the left of the Presidential car, on a grey horse. Soon the white *chhatri* itself is visible, and then Parliament House of the Parliament House, a perfect symmetry of architecture surrounded by lush green trees, the seat of the largest democracy in the world.

The Presidential car stops and the two most important people of the day alight at the gate, received by Lok Sabha Speaker Somnath Chatterjee, Chief Justice K.G. Balakrishnan, and Chairman of the Rajya Sabha K. Rahman Khan. After President Kalam takes the salute of the Presidential guard, he and Ms Patil alight the maroon carpeted steps, then walk over the red carpet to Central Hall, led by two uniformed men in a slow, ceremonial march. President Kalam in front, waving to the people, Ms Patil behind. The call of the bugle in the background, they enter the hall, smiling and nodding, and soon you can just about catch a glimpse of *pallu* over several male heads.

They ascend the steps to their high-backed seats of a sober green leather and wooden frame. Standing at attention to the strains of the national anthem, their expressions are strikingly similar – straight, direct looks, lips closed, cheeks slightly in. The *Jana Gana Mana* ... over, they are seated – President Kalam on the left and Ms Patil on the right. The proceedings begin. First there is the reading of the result at the polls, and some applause. Then, the first Dalit Chief Justice of India, Shri K.G. Balakrishnan, administers the Presidential oath to the first woman President, Ms Pratibha Patil, who rises to stand before the mike. Her voice rings out firm and clear as she repeats after him, "I, Pratibha Devisingh Patil, do solemnly affirm to execute the office of President of India and will, to the best of my ability...". As the pledge is completed, Central Hall resounds with the applause of the audience. The oath is sealed with the signing of the register by the new President, below whose signature is that of the Secretary to the President. Now former President Kalam and the first woman President of India, Ms Pratibha Devisingh Patil, exchange a *Namaste* and their seats – the former on the left and latter on the right as the 21n salute booms in the background.

After the reading of the functions of President, the new President rises to read out her maiden address to the nation, first in English and then in Hindi. "I stand here as the republic's first servant and I will endeavour to live up to the high expectations from this office to serve the best interests of the people." Thanking the legislators for electing her, she recalled the contribution of all those who had participated in the struggle for freedom, in which both men and women had played an equal part. She reiterated her belief that empowerment of women would lead to the empowerment of the nation. Mentioning the contribution of Begum Hazrat Mahal, and quoting Marathi poet Sant Tukaram and Rabindranath Tagore, the new President said, "All of us should re-dedicate ourselves to work for the betterment of the lives of the poor for a future in which every Indian will hold his head high."

As she read on to the end, one got a brief glimpse of the *mangalsutra* around the neck of India's first lady President...JAI HIND.

12

Patil and Clinton

I think the key is for women not to set any limits.
—Martina Navratilova

12

Considering that women make up half the population of the world, very few of them actually make it to positions of decision-making and power. Those who do are notable exceptions. According to a recent survey, on an average, only eleven per cent women are included in the legislatures of the world, of which a third or more are in six-odd countries and none in some countries in the Middle East.

The first decade of the twenty-first century may well prove to be the women's decade for the world's two largest democracies—India and the United States of America. In case of India, Pratibha Patil has already been elected to the highest office of the President of the country—the first Indian woman to do so. Whether similar history will be created in the US remains to be seen, as Hillary Rodham Clinton, a prominent Democratic contender for the post of President of USA for 2008 makes her way through the political rites of passages.

Interestingly, there are many similarities in the personal and political lives of Pratibha Patil and Hillary Clinton. Both were born into politically conservative families with progressive views regarding the education and careers of daughters. In both the cases, the fathers were a major influence in the lives of their daughters.

It is amazing how their lives have also taken similar turns at different stages. Hillary was a keen participant in sports in her schooldays, earning awards as a Brownie and Girl Scout, while Pratibha won laurels for her college in table-tennis and other sports. The two, as young girls, though separated across nations and seas, were all-rounders, Hillary being active in the student council and debating team while Pratibha became College Queen and was known for her impressive speeches. While Hillary volunteered for Republican candidate Barry Goldwater in the US presidential election of 1964, Pratibha enthusiastically championed the Congress candidate and her mentor, Y.S. Mahajan, in Jalgaon at about the same time.

Both are married to men who have been in positions of political power – Bill Clinton having been Governor of Arkansas and President of the US, and Devisingh Shekhawat the mayor of Amravati. It's also a coincidence how they have chosen to retain their maiden names even after marriage. The only difference being that while the first citizen of India keeps her husband's name in the middle and maiden name last – Pratibha Devisingh Patil, the former first lady of the US keeps it the other way round – Hillary Rodham Clinton.

It has to be more than coincidence that both began their careers in law in the 1970s! They even had similar political ideals. While Pratibha was a staunch supporter and admirer of Indira Gandhi, Hillary looked up to Martin Luther King Jr., and as a student was much affected by his death. Another uncanny similarity is the progress of their political careers. Pratibha Patil has never lost a single election, and Hillary Clinton has consistently been the front-runner in polls for the Democratic nomination.

Even the firsts of their lives are closely related. Pratibha Patil was the first woman Governor of Rajasthan. Hillary Rodham Clinton was elected to the United States Senate in 2000, becoming the first First Lady elected to public office and the first woman elected Senator from New York.

Both are champions of cause of women education and empowerment, and the welfare of children.

Keeping up the list, the crises in their lives too seem to have run along similar tracks. There has been mudslinging against both, without any of the allegations having been proved. In 1996 Hillary became the first First Lady to be subpoenaed to testify before a Federal grand jury, on account of the Whitewater scandal; however, she was never charged with any wrongdoing in this or several other investigations while her husband was President.

When Pratibha Patil was nominated for President, there were rumours of misappropriation of funds, involvement of her brother in murder, her statements regarding the purdah system, visitations of Dada Lekhraj...allegations that she has chosen to ignore and remain silent about.

Strangely enough, none of the alleged charges were raked up when she was stepping into the office of Governor of Rajasthan, and a head of a state is as close as one can get to becoming head of the nation. When one is in the limelight, there are bound to be some shadows cast as well.

13

Women in Power

The true worth of a race must be measured by the character of its womanhood.

—Mary McLeod Bethune

13

As far as heads of state go, history unveils an interesting fact. While many of the larger and economically more developed countries – the US, Russia, Spain, Australia - have never had a woman head of state, a considerable number of smaller developed, developing and Third World countries have had many such firsts.

For instance, the People's Great Khural of Mongolia's First Deputy Chairman of its Presidium, as well as acting Chairman was Suhbaataryn Yanjma, widow of national hero Suhbaatar, from September 1953 to July 1954. This makes her, with the exception of queens, the absolute first woman political ruler in contemporary history.

In China, Song Qingling shared de facto presidential duties with Dong Biwu from 1968 to 1972. Just before her death, in 1980, she was elected Honorary President of the People's Republic of China.

Argentina has the distinction of having the first woman President in the world. Also the first to be ousted in a military coup, Maria Estela ('Isabel') Martinez de Peron was President of Argentina from 1 July 1974 to 24 March 1976.

Continuing the trend, in Bolivia, Lydia Gueiler Tejada served as caretaker president from 17 November 1979 to 18 July 1980, and was deposed in a military coup.

Apart from the Presidential chair, there have been many iron ladies in the Prime Minister's chair as well. The term Iron Lady is actually a nickname that has frequently been used to describe female heads of government around the world. Describing a "strong willed" woman, this metaphor was most famously applied to Margaret Thatcher in 1976 by the Soviet media for her staunch opposition to communism. Margaret Thatcher was the longest-serving British Prime Minister (from 1979 to 1990) since Lord Salisbury and had the longest continuous period in office since Lord Liverpool who was prime minister in the early 19th century.

Other leaders who have earned this unofficial title include late Indira Gandhi, who was Prime Minister of India from 1966 to 1977, and again from 1980 to 1984. A commanding personality, she had a rather controversial administration, and used the military to put an end to a Sikh separatist operation, which led to her assassination by her Sikh security guards in 1984.

Golda Meir, the Prime Minister of Israel from 1969 to 1974, and Barbara Castle, a British left-wing politician (1910-2002) were also considered women of power in their own right.

Golda Meir, one of the founders of the State of Israel, served as the fourth and, thus far, only female Prime Minister of her country from 11 March 1969 to 3 June 1974. She was also the third female Prime Minister in the world. She came to be known as the Iron Lady of Israeli politics years before the term was used for Margaret Thatcher. In fact, Israel's first Prime Minister, David Ben-Gurion, once referred to her as "the only man in the Cabinet!"

Closer home is the example of Pakistan's Benazir Bhutto, mentioned as "the world's most popular politician" in the Guinness Book of Records 1996, and listed as one among the 100 most powerful women by the Times and The Australian Magazine the same year. Benazir became active in politics after her father, late Pakistani Prime Minister Zulfikar Ali Bhutto was ousted from office in a military coup in 1977 and later executed. Overcoming government persecution and lack of political experience, Benazir led her Pakistan People's Party to victory in the parliamentary elections of November 1988 and October 1993.

In 2006, the Forbes magazine ranked Khaleda Zia amongst the 100 most powerful women in the world. Khaleda Zia was Prime Minister of

Bangladesh from 1991 to 1996, the first woman in the country's history to hold that position, and then again from 2001 to 2006. Widow of assassinated President of Bangladesh, Zia-ur Rahman, she leads his old party, the Bangladesh Nationalist Party. In thirty-five years of independence of Bangladesh, she has ruled the country for about ten years (the longest period), and been elected to five separate parliamentary constituencies in the general elections of 1991, 1996, and 2001, a feat unachieved by any other politician in Bangladeshi history.

Sheikh Hasina, daughter of the founding father of Bangladesh, Bangabandhu Sheikh Mujibur Rahman, was sworn in as the tenth Prime Minister on June 2, 1996, restoring democracy after twenty-one years of ruthless oppression, free-wheeling corruption and overt and covert martial law. In 1975, her father and members of her family were cruelly assassinated, but Hasina and her sister Sheikh Rehana had a lucky escape as they were out of the country. Despite being forced to remain outside, Hasina continued to work for uniting the Bangladeshis at home and abroad. On May 17, 1981 after nearly six years in exile, Sheikh Hasina returned to Bangladesh as the President of Bangladesh Awami League, at the young age of 33.

Our next-door neighbour, Sri Lanka, holds the unique position of being the first republic in the world whose two top executive offices were simultaneously held by women, both posts having been filled through democratic elections. Chandrika

Kumaratunga was elected President and her mother became Prime Minister in December 1994. Prior to that in 1960 her mother, Sirimavo Bandaranaike, was Prime Minister.

Vigdis Finnbogadottir, was President of Iceland from 1 August 1980 to 1 August 1996, and was the first: woman president in Europe, elected directly by the people in the world.

The second woman president in Europe was Agatha Barbara of Malta, from 15 February 1982 to 15 February 1987.

Not to be left behind, Asia saw its first woman president in Corazon (Cory) Aquino, widow of Benigno Aquino. She presided over the Philippines from 25 February 1986 to 30 June 1992.

The third female president and second black female ruler in the American continent was Dame Ertha Pascal-Druillot, who was interim president of Haiti from 13 March 1990 to 7 February 1991.

Just before East and West Germany united, the last head of state of the German Democratic Republic was Sabine Bergmann-Pohl, who served for six months as Chairman of the Volkshammer. She was also the only female head of state in the former communist East Europe. Currently, Germany has a woman chancellor, Angela Dorothea Merkel.

Mary Robinson, who later became United Nations High Commissioner for Human Rights, was President of Ireland from 3 December 1990 to 12 September 1997.

Yet another first was Ruth Perry, Africa's first female head of State.

The first woman to become Swiss head of state as president of the Confederation was Ruth Dreifuss, who was elected by the Federal Assembly and had a tenure from 1 January 1999 to 1 January 2000.

It's quite a series of firsts actually, and more women than we know have left their footprints on the political sands of time. Vaire Vike-Freiberga, the first woman to be president of a country in East/Central Europe was elected by the Parliament of Latvia on 17 June 1999 for a four-year term. The first woman president of Panama, Mireya Elisa Moscoso de Arias, served from 1 September 1999 to 1 September 2004. Tarja Kaarina Halonen, Finland's first woman president, stepped into office on 1 March 2000. Ellen Johnson-Sirleaf, President of Liberia since 16 January 2006, holds the honour of being Africa's first elected woman president. Michelle Bachelet Jeria became President of Chile on 11 March 2006. Then we have Micheline Calmy-Rey, who is President of the Swiss Confederation for the annual period 1 January 2007 to 1 January 2008. Dalia Itzik took over as acting president of the State of Israel on 25 January 2007, when the incumbent office-holder, Moshe Katzav, went on a-three month leave of absence to deal with criminal charges.

Thus, despite being small in number, women have been ruling the political stage, and leaving their mark.

A champion of women empowerment, Pratibha Patil believes, "If all the rivers of the world come together, what a great river it will be. If all the trees of the world are joined together what a great three it will be. If all the women in the world speak in one voice, what a great voice it will be."

14

A Defining Moment

Nothing is so strong as gentleness. Nothing is so gentle as real strength.

—Irences de Sales

14

Succeeding Dr APJ Abdul Kalam–who has by far proved to be the most popular President in the sixty years of India's independent existence–can be a daunting task for even the most accomplished and seasoned politician. Known as the People's President, he leaves behind a legacy that would be difficult to match, leave alone surpass. As if that were not enough, the fact that the succeeding President is a woman will ensure that the spotlight would be focused more searingly and searchingly on her than on any of her predecessors.

How will Pratibha Patil live up to the expectations that the people now have of the President's office? Even after taking on the mantle of President, she appears unfazed by any pressures and expectations, retaining her usual cool demeanour. Setting aside any misgivings that she would be a President in name only, she firmly replies, "Forget about that. I am not going to be a rubber stamp President–look at my record," obviously referring to her refusal to sign the Freedom of Religion Bill and her unwillingness to yield to the Congress's clamouring for imposition of President's Rule during the Gujjar agitation in May-June 2007, when she was Governor of Rajasthan.

That she is very much a woman with a definite mind and style of her own, who knows how to walk the tightrope—equally balancing political compulsions and the dignity of the President's office—was made clear when she met the BJP delegation from Goa just a few days after assuming office. The delegation drew her attention to the prevailing political confusion in the state and wanted some sort of assurance of intervention from her. She met them, offered words of sympathy and cups of tea but no promises, making it clear that this was a matter for the state government.

This action—and her earlier ones as Governor—make it clear that her guiding force would be the Constitution. In her own words, "The Constitution says it all—the rules of the various organs of the state, the executive, the judiciary and legislature are well-defined. I will just be guided by the Constitution."

With the Constitution as her guiding light and her philosophy of *'nishkam bhakti'* (devotion to God without any desire), the twelfth President's term may well turn out be a defining moment in the history of the nation, for reasons beyond gender alone.

❑❑❑

Political Profile of Pratibha Patil

* Member of Maharashtra Legislative Assembly : 1962-85
* Deputy Minister, Public Health, Prohibition, Tourism, Housing and Parliamentary Affairs, Govt. of Maharashtra : 1967-72
* Cabinet Minister, Social Welface, Govt. of Maharashtra : 1972-74
* Cabinet Minister, Public Health and Social Welfare, Maharashtra : 1973-74
* Cabinet Minister, Prohibition, Rehabilitation and Cultural Affairs, Govt. of Maharashtra : 1975-76
* Cabinet Minister, Education, Govt. of Maharashtra : 1977-78
* Leader of Opposition, CLP (I), Govt. of Maharashtra : 1979-80
* Cabinet Minister, Urban Development and Housing, Govt. of Maharashtra : 1982-85
* Cabinet Minister, Civil Supplies and Social Welfare, Govt. of Maharashtra : 1983-85
* Member of Rajya Sabha : 1985-90.
* Deputy Chairman, Rajya Sabha : 1986-88.
* Chairman, Committee on Privileges, Rajya Sabha Member, Business Advisory Committee, Rajya Sabha : 1986-88
* Member of 10th Lok Sabha : 1991-96,
* Governor of Rajasthan : 8 November 2004-22 June 2007.
* President of India : 25 July 2007.

Bibliography

Information has been taken from :
India Today, July 9, 2007
Outlook, July 2, 2007
Outlook, August 13, 2007
www.wikipedia.com
www.nilacharal.com
www.timesofindia.com
www.sulekha.com
www.womenshistory.about.com
Interview on Doordarshan

Read these Bestsellers by Dr. APJ Abdul Kalam

Rs. 350/-

Indomitable Spirit
by **Dr. APJ Abdul Kalam**

By far the most popular political public figure in recent times, Dr. Kalam is today known as the 'Peoples President'. In his five years as President of the country, he has fired the imagination of the people with his vision for a Developed India.

'Indomitable Spirit' brings together his values, thoughts, ideas and ideals and is interspersed with interesting anecodotes.

Rs. 150/-

Inspiring Thoughts
A selection of the best of APJ Abdul Kalam's thought–provoking and inspiring words: words which will make you reflect, rethink and rejoice along this journey of life.

An Inspiring Read! An Ideal Gift!

Available at all major booksellers
Or log on to
www.rajpalsons.com

or write to us at
Rajpal & Sons
1590 Madarsa Road, Kashmere Gate, Delhi-110 006
email : mail@rajplsons.com